Afforestation In Great Britain And Ireland

William Schlich

In the interest of creating a more extensive selection of rare historical book reprints, we have chosen to reproduce this title even though it may possibly have occasional imperfections such as missing and blurred pages, missing text, poor pictures, markings, dark backgrounds and other reproduction issues beyond our control. Because this work is culturally important, we have made it available as a part of our commitment to protecting, preserving and promoting the world's literature. Thank you for your understanding.

AFFORESTATION

IN

GREAT BRITAIN AND IRELAND.

BY

W. SCHLICH, Ph.D.

DUBLIN:
PRINTED BY ALEX. THOM & CO. (Limited), 87, 88, & 89, ABBEY-ST.,
THE QUEEN'S PRINTING OFFICE.

1886.

CONTENTS.

	Page
INTRODUCTION,	5
I.—GENERAL CONSIDERATIONS,	7
1. Direct Effects of Forests,	8
2. Indirect Effects of Forests,	8
3. Area of Forests,	9
4. Forests as objects of Industry,	13
5. Forest Revenue,	15
6. Summary of Conclusions,	16
II.—THE AFFORESTATION OF IRELAND,	17
1. Forests in relation to Topography and Drainage,	17
2. ,, ,, Climate,	20
3. ,, ,, Winds,	22
4. ,, ,, Wood Production,	22
5. ,, ,, Labour,	23
6. Area available for Forests in Ireland,	26
7. Organization,	29
8. A few Sylvicultural Notes,	30

INTRODUCTION.

THE question of afforestation in Great Britain and Ireland has, for some years past, received special attention. Various papers have been published setting forth the inadequacy of the British woodlands, and the uncertainty which prevails as regards future supplies of timber. Dr. Robert Lyons, late member of Parliament for Dublin, has specially taken up the afforestation of Ireland, as he believes that it will act beneficially in various respects. The Select Committee of the House of Commons on Industries (Ireland) investigated the question, and examined Mr. D. Howitz, whose evidence will be found at pages 253-295 of the Report of the Select Committee, printed by order of the House of Commons in July, 1885. Another Select Committee of the House of Commons was appointed last summer, on the motion of Sir John Lubbock, member of Parliament for the University of London, with the object of considering whether, by the establishment of a Forest School or otherwise, the British woodlands could be rendered more remunerative. This Committee examined Mr. William G. Pedder, Colonel James Michael, C.S.I., Dr. Hugh Cleghorn, Colonel G. Pearson, Mr. W. T. Thiselton Dyer, C.M.G., and Mr. Julian C. Rogers, whose evidence is recorded in the Report of the Committee, printed by order of the House of Commons in July, 1885.

I have, during the last six months, visited various parts of Great Britain and Ireland in connexion with the establishment of an Indian Forest School at the Royal Indian Engineering College, Coopers Hill, and I have been strongly urged to give my views on the question of afforestation, especially with reference to Ireland. Although I have not yet seen enough to deal with this large subject in detail, I propose to offer a few remarks in so far as personal inspection and past experience in my profession in Europe and India justify me in doing. If the question should arrive at a practical issue it will be necessary to investigate it in much greater detail, than has yet been done.

AFFORESTATION

IN

GREAT BRITAIN AND IRELAND.

I.—GENERAL CONSIDERATIONS.

Forests are, in the economy of nature and of man, of direct and indirect value; the former through their products, and the latter through the influence which they exercise upon climate, the regulation of the water supply, the healthiness of a country, and allied subjects. The principal points are, without going into full detail, the following:—

(1.) Forests supply timber, fuel, and other forest products.

(2.) They provide work, and tend to produce a variety of industries.

(3.) They tend to reduce the temperature of the soil and the air, and to render the climate more equable.

(4.) They increase the relative humidity of the air, and probably reduce evaporation.

(5.) They tend to increase the rainfall.

(6.) They regulate the water supply, insure a more sustained yield of springs, reduce the violence of sudden floods, and render the flow of water in rivers more continuous.

(7.) They prevent landslips, the formation of avalanches, the silting up of rivers, and they arrest moving sand.

(8.) They reduce the velocity of winds, and afford protection to adjoining fields.

(9.) They afford shelter to cattle and to useful birds.

(10.) They assist in the production of oxygen, and especially of ozone.

(11.) They may, under certain conditions, improve the healthiness of a country, and, under others, reduce it.

(12.) Finally, they increase the artistic beauty of a country.

2. It is not intended to give here the details upon which these conclusions rest; I hope to do this on another occasion, and I shall now only state that nothing has been included in the above twelve points which is not supported by accurate observations,

1. *Direct Effects of Forests.*

3. As regards the direct effects of forests, mentioned above under first and second, the most important points for consideration are:—

- (*a.*) The position of a country, its communications with other countries, and the control exercised by one country over others.
- (*b.*) The quality and quantity of substitutes for forest products available in a country.
- (*c.*) The value of land and labour, and the return which land yields as field, grass-land, or forest, respectively.
- (*d.*) The density of population of a country.

4. A country so situated that the importation of wood and other forest products is comparatively easy and cheap (sea-bound, or traversed by navigable rivers coming from a country rich in forests, or intersected by numerous railways and other means of communication), or which has control over other countries, especially colonies, rich in forests, can dispense with extensive forests. In a country which is rich in coal, lignite, or peat, the production of firewood is of subordinate importance. Where iron or other substitutes for timber in sufficient quantity and at a low rate are available, forests are not required to the same extent as in a country which does not enjoy such advantages. Where land under cereals or grass yields, even if forest produce is imported, more valuable returns (higher interest on capital) than under forest, the latter would, in this respect, be out of place. If the population of a country is very dense, and all land is required for the production of food, forests will not find a place. Where, on the other hand, waste lands exist which are not required or unsuited for cultivation and grass-lands, and where the population is in want of additional work, it may be advisable to create forests, and thus provide occupation through the operations connected with the administration of the forests and the industries, which the existence of forests tends to create.

2. *Indirect Effects of Forests.*

5. In considering the indirect effects of forests, the most important factors are the climate and configuration of a country. The nearer to the equator, the more important becomes, as a rule, the forest question, and the further north the less important. While forests may in a hot country, with distinct wet and dry seasons, be absolutely necessary for the mitigation of extreme heat and dryness during certain parts of the year, and the regulation of the flow of water in springs and rivers, they may be injurious in a northern country, which is already too cold and damp. Similarly, a continental country may require forests, while a sea-bound country may be better without them, as far as climatic considerations are concerned. A mountainous country is much more in need of forests than a level country, on account

of their beneficial action as regards landslips, avalanches, the carrying away of debris, the silting up of rivers and low lands, sudden floods, and the sustained feeding of springs. The action in this respect is produced in the following manner :—

(1.) The branches and leaves of the trees break the force of the falling rain, and retain a portion of it which evaporates.

(2.) The covering of forest soil and the roots of the trees prevent the gliding down of earth and rock, and the formation of avalanches on hill sides.

(3.) The covering of forest soil (humus or leaf-mould, mosses, shrubs, &c.,) possesses in a high degree the faculty of absorbing water and of retaining it for a time. It has, for instance, been proved that mosses of the genus Hypnum absorb three and a half to five times their weight of water, and peat mosses of the genus Sphagnum even nine times their weight, while the leaf-mould found in a middle-aged, well-stocked and well-preserved beech forest is capable of retaining, for a time, five inches of rain. The water thus absorbed reduces the quantity which rushes down sloping ground during rain; it partly penetrates into the ground, and the rest is slowly given up. Well-preserved forests, with a good layer of leaf-mould, act, therefore, like huge water reservoirs, which increase the quantity of water penetrating the soil, and which render the flow of water in rivers less fluctuating.

6. As regards the protection against strong winds, and shelter to cattle and useful birds, forests act beneficially in any country.

7. In applying these facts to Great Britain and Ireland it should be remembered, that the climate and rainfall of these countries is principally governed by their insular position, which exposes them to strong air currents coming direct from the sea. Compared with their effects, those of forests, even if they occupied twenty per cent. of the total area, would be comparatively small. Again, by far the greater portion of the waste lands in Great Britain and Ireland is covered with heath, and a considerable portion with peat mosses, which are most powerful agents in the retention of water; moreover afforestation would, in many cases, be accompanied by the draining of the soil, which would counteract the effects of forests; hence afforestation in these islands would not produce, comparatively, the same effect, as in a country where unafforested soil has generally no covering.

3. *Area of Forests.*

8. No general rule can be laid down showing whether forests are required in a country, or what percentage of the area should be so stocked. The forest question must be determined on the special circumstances of each country. Dr. Lyons published a

short time ago a statement showing the latest estimates of the forest areas in a number of countries, which I reproduce below. Some of the data require confirmation, but on the whole they give a fair idea of the areas. I have added two columns showing the percentage of the total area of each country under forest, and the forest area per head of population :—

Country.	Area in Square Miles.		Per-centage of Total Area under Forest.	Area of Forest per Head of Population, in Statute Acres.
	Total.	Under Forest.		
Russia in Europe,	1,944,324	824,104	42	6·1
Sweden,	157,055	66,197	42	9·1
Austria Proper,	108,420	36,376	34	} 1·2
Hungary,	130,008	35,179	27	
Germany,	207,931	53,409	26	0·8
Norway,	119,870	29,563	25	9·9
France,	203,996	35,450	17	0·6
Belgium,	11,376	1,677	15	0·2
Italy,	114,362	14,111	12	0·3
Holland,	12,515	832	7	0·1
Denmark,	13,396	623	5	0·2
Great Britain and Ireland,	120,312*	4,360†	4	0·1
Total,	3,143,565	1,101,881	35	—
United States of America,	3,580,242	593,750	17	7·6

9. It has been estimated that the percentage of land under forest required for a country situated and populated like the centre of Germany, may be put down at about 25 per cent. of the total area. Judging by this standard, and assuming that the data given in the above table are approximately correct, it would appear that Russia and Sweden have as yet more land under forest, than is absolutely required. Denmark and Great Britain and Ireland have a very small percentage of land under forest, but they are not only sea-bound, but also situated under a northern latitude, and it would be premature to conclude at first sight, that their forest areas are too small.

10. Great Britain and Ireland are well supplied with coal and peat, and the production of firewood is of very little importance; as a matter of fact, firewood is unsaleable in many parts of the country. The question of the supply of timber requires a more detailed notice. Although the production of iron is enormous, the imports of wood into Great Britain and Ireland are stated to

* This is the figure given by Dr. Lyons; it does not quite agree with those found further on.
† Dr. Lyons gives only 4,009 square miles; he has apparently omitted the woodlands of Wales.

have amounted in 1883 to 6,447,211* loads. For the same year the value of home production and imports of forest produce are given, in round figures, as follows:—

	£
Estimated value of wood produced in the country,	3,000,000
Value of imported wood,	18,000,000
Total value of wood,	21,000,000
Value of minor† forest produce, as bark, dye woods, wood pulp, galls, turpentine, pitch and tar, resin, lac, gum, caoutchouc, gutta percha, fibres, &c., imported,	14,000,000
Grand Total,	£35,000,000

The total value is equivalent to about one pound per head of population, per annum.

11. It appears that of the total quantity of timber required by the country, only about one-seventh (according to value), is produced at home. If the whole of the required timber were to be grown locally, it would be necessary to increase the area under forest to about 20 per cent. of the total area of the country, or, say, to 24,000 square miles. A considerable portion of the imports consists, however, of teak, fancy woods, &c., which could not be grown in these islands. Still, after making allowance for these, an area of about 20,000 square miles, or nearly five times the present area, would be required.

12. The question of the future timber supply comes to this:— "Is it necessary or advisable to increase the area under forest in Great Britain and Ireland, with the view of meeting future requirements of timber, or can colonies and other countries be relied on to meet the demand"? This question has been extensively discussed of late, and I shall restrict my remarks to the most obvious point, the supply of those ordinary kinds of timber, which will readily grow in the climate of these islands.

13. Of the 6,447,211 loads of wood imported in 1883, the following quantities came from the more important sources:—

	Loads.
From Sweden,	1,600,000
,, Russia,	1,350,000
,, Norway,	750,000
,, Germany,	430,000
,, The United States of America,	400,000
Total,	4,530,000
Canada,	1,540,000
Grand Total,	6,070,000

In round figures, Great Britain and Ireland received one and a half million loads from the Dominion of Canada, over which

---

* Simmons, in the *Journal of the Society of Arts*, 19th December, 1884.
† In Forest terminology, *major produce* means wood (timber and firewood); *minor produce*, all other articles obtained from forests.

the Government of this country has a certain control, and four and a half million loads from countries over which it has no control. Although these data refer only to one year, 1883, they approximate to the average imports of the last five years sufficiently close for the present argument. As far as the available information goes, it seems almost certain, that the supply from the United States of America will die away at an early date, thus reducing the available quantity by 400,000 tons. Of the foregoing European States a sustained yield is at present only secured from Germany, where the bulk of the forests is under systematic management and control ; indeed, it is believed that the imports can easily be increased, especially from the forests in East Prussia. In Sweden, Norway, and Russia, the forest conservancy measures so far introduced do not, if I am correctly informed, ensure a sustained yield of the quantities removed of late years, though the falling off in the supplies may not be so rapid as has been assumed. These sources, then, cannot be relied on to furnish for any length of time 3,700,000 loads annually, or more than one half of the total imports, even if the supplies from Germany should somewhat increase. None of the other large European countries will materially help to cover the deficiency, any surplus material available in Austria being required by France and other countries.

14. Canada has sent about one and a half million loads annually, but gloomy reports have been received of the extensive destruction of forests in that country. The matter is said to receive now attention, and if, as has been stated, the area of timber lands has been reduced to less than ten per cent. of the total area, it is high time to take energetic steps towards the introduction of proper forest conservancy measures and the reproduction of the forests. Large areas, otherwise not required, are available for the purpose, and the Government of England should use all possible influence to bring about the setting aside for forest purposes of suitable areas on a large scale.

15. In how far South America and Africa can make good any deficiency of timber in Europe, is not known at present. Australia can probably do very little in this respect. The imports from India have hitherto been restricted to that of teak (maximum 45,000 loads) and of a small quantity of fancy woods. As the price of timber rises, with decreasing supplies, other kinds of useful timber may be added, but the expenses will always be comparatively high, apart from the fact, that India is likely to require as much timber as it produces.

16. On the whole, although I am far from joining those who would create a panic on the timber supply question, there is every prospect, that any woods now planted in Great Britain and Ireland will yield a fair return, by the time that they are ripe for the axe. At present prices are very low, but that should not induce the present generation to disregard the future. Wood is an article which requires a long time to mature, and forethought as regards future supplies of it is more necessary, than in respect of any other article.

17. From the Agricultural Statistics of 1884 and 1885, I gather that the area of Great Britain and Ireland is distributed as follows:—

Division of Land.	Area in square miles.				Per-centage of total area.			
	England and Wales.	Scotland.	Ireland.	Total.	England and Wales.	Scotland.	Ireland.	Total.
Under crops, including meadows, orchards, gardens, and grass lands.	43,687	7,585	23,818	75,090	74·9	24·9	73·2	61·9
Woods and forests,	2,545	1,296	519	4,360	4·4	4·3	1·6	3·6
Barren mountain land, bog, marsh, waste land, roads, water, fences, &c.	12,079	21,536	8,194	41,809	20·7	70·8	25·2	34·5
Grand total,	58,311	30,417	32,531	121,259*	100	100	100	100

The Director-General of the Ordnance Survey has kindly furnished me with the following figures:—

England and Wales,	59,469	square miles.
Scotland,	30,902	,,
Ireland,	32,531	,,
Total,	122,902	,,

These figures include all water and foreshores.

The total area of all waste lands amounts to 41,809 square miles. I am not in a position to state, at present, what proportion of this area is fit and available for forests, but on the whole it may perhaps be estimated at one-half, or 20,000 square miles, in round figures. At any rate it is evident that there is sufficient room for a considerable extension of the woodlands in Great Britain and Ireland.

4. *Forests as objects of Industry.*

18. Forests are important objects of industry; they require labour in their creation, preservation and the removal of the produce. A great variety of occupations depend on the products of forests as their prime materials—not only as regards construction, manufacture, furniture making, &c., and the industries using minor forest produce, which would be in existence in any case, whether the material is imported or produced locally—but also as regards special industries, which cannot spring into existence except in and around large forests with a sustained and regular yield. The articles produced by the latter are now mostly imported, but they could, to a considerable extent, be made by local labour, if Great Britain and Ireland had extensive forests.

* This is the area given in the Agricultural Statistics.

19. The quantity of labour required for forest operations varies with the value of the products, and the consequent greater or less minuteness of the system of management. The number of persons required for the ordinary work in the forests, administration, creation, preservation, cutting of wood, and collection of minor products, has, for forests situated like those of Germany, been variously estimated at one adult labourer for every 100 to 500 English acres. This estimate refers to forests already in existence, in which, perhaps, one per cent. of the area is annually cleared and restocked, and a great portion of which is of small value. For Great Britain and Ireland it may be assumed, that about one adult labourer will be required for every 100 acres, after the forests have been created; while the initial planting work is going on, about every 15 to 20 acres would supply work for one labourer throughout the year, what with preparation of the soil, draining, nursery work, planting, sowing, fencing, &c. Assuming that the forest area of Great Britain and Ireland were, during the next 20 years, increased from 4,360 to 20,000 square miles, it would be necessary to plant annually some 500,000 acres, which would fully occupy at least 25,000 labourers, corresponding to a population of 125,000 people. After the forests had been created, they would give employment to about 100,000 labourers, corresponding to a population of half a million. Large as these figures are, it will be seen, that forests give but small employment when compared with agriculture, and it follows that, ordinarily, all lands required for agriculture could, as regards the labour question, not be made available for forests. The latter must be restricted to surplus areas or to lands not suited for agriculture, as long as the forest products are obtainable at a reasonable rate from outside sources.

20. Before leaving this subject, the following information may find a place here:—Prussia, Bavaria, Saxony, Wurtemberg, Baden, and Alsace-Lorraine, have a combined population of 40,644,736 people. The labour connected with the forests of these countries, and their products, has been estimated to be worth:—

	£
Labour in the forests,	4,550,000
Carriage of wood, etc.,	3,900,000
Collection of minor products,	1,000,000
Total,	9,450,000

These earnings suffice for the maintenance of about 300,000 families, or one and a half million people. It has further been estimated that the prime material yielded by the forests occupies about four millions people, so that forests and industries dependent on them provide work for some seven millions people, or one-sixth of the total population of the above mentioned countries.

5. *Forest Revenue.*

21. Although it is not intended to discuss here in full detail the revenue obtainable from forests, it will not be out of place to offer a few remarks on the subject. It has been put forward, from various quarters, that forests in England can be made to pay better than land under cultivation. This may be the case under very special conditions, but generally I do not believe it to be possible. Data have been produced showing that land under forest has yielded higher returns than would have been obtained by letting the land for agricultural purposes, but in these cases it has generally been overlooked, that the return in the one case represents the interest on a much higher capital than in the other. I shall do best to explain this by an example, which I shall, for convenience sake, make as simple as possible. Assuming that certain land yields, if let for agriculture, 6s. an acre a year; the purchase value of this land would be £10 an acre, calculating with 3 per cent., and this is the capital of which 6s. represents the annual interest. If the land is, instead of letting it, put under forest, it will yield no return for a series of years, and, in addition, a certain sum must be spent in creating the forest; both items with their compound interest must be added to the invested capital. Ordinarily newly created forests must be closed for, say, thirty years, during which time they yield little or no return. Assuming that the returns from thinnings made between the thirtieth and fiftieth year cover the expense of maintenance for the whole fifty years and that the full returns commence with the fiftieth year, a most favourable and rare case, the account would stand as follows, at the end of fifty years:—

Value of land, per acre, with compound interest at three per cent. for fifty years—

	£	s.	d.
$S = 10 \times 1 \cdot 03^{50}$	43	16	9

Value of outlay on the creation of the forest, say £3 per acre—

$S = 3 \times 1 \cdot 03^{50}$	13	3	0
Total,	56	19	9

In a round sum, £57 represents the forest capital, and if the concern is to yield three per cent. on the invested capital, the returns from the forest must amount to £1 14s. 2d. an acre a year, or nearly six times the rent obtainable by letting the land. Except under very special circumstances (osier beds &c.), such returns will not be obtained, and I am satisfied that, ordinarily land fit for cultivation will, if used in this way, yield higher interest on the invested capital, than if stocked with wood.

22. I have experienced great difficulty in obtaining reliable data regarding the returns obtained from forests in Great Britain and Ireland. Inquiries made by me seem, however, to show, that the great forest estates in Scotland do at present not yield, on the

whole, more than about five shillings an acre, which, at three per cent. interest and according to the above assumptions, corresponds to an average purchase value of the land equal to £1 10s. an acre, or an annual land revenue of about 11d. an acre. Some of the lands are, perhaps, not worth more, some even less, but the average value is decidedly higher, and a good portion would yield ten and twenty times eleven pence a year, if let for agricultural purposes. The above mentioned return of five shillings an acre does not include the receipts which some of the Scotch proprietors at present obtain by letting the land for deer shooting, but that is, it seems to me, a somewhat abnormal source of income, which may disappear as suddenly as it has sprung into existence.

23. It may be contended, that the price of timber is very low at present, and that it may and probably will rise as trade revives and foreign supplies of timber become exhausted. That may be so, but other items may also change, and it would be undesirable to rest a calculation on uncertain future events.

6. Summary of Conclusions.

24. In summing up these general considerations, the following principal conclusions may be drawn in respect of Great Britain and Ireland :—

(1.) As the imports of wood and other forest produce are very great, and as it is doubtful whether sufficient supplies can be permanently obtained from other countries, the extension of the home forest area can be strongly recommended, provided it is carried out on surplus lands. The additional wood-lands may safely be expected to yield fair returns on the invested capital, if the work of creation and administration of the forests is done in an economic manner.

(2.) The surplus area is so great, that extensive tracts can be set aside for forests, without trenching on the land required for agriculture (fields and grass lands).

(3.) The tendency of the forests to reduce the temperature of the soil and the air, to increase the relative humidity of the air and the rainfall, is of subordinate importance in these islands, which are, owing to their geographical and sea-bound position, subject to influences, in comparison with which those of forests are small.

(4.) The increase of the forest area will act very beneficially in reducing the effects of winds on adjoining lands under cultivation, and in affording shelter to cattle and useful birds.

(5.) The extension of the area under forest will provide additional work, without interfering with existing sources of occupation.

I am not at present prepared to go beyond what has been stated in the above five points, but I believe it to be sufficient to show, that a fair field for judicious enterprise exists in the extension of the wood-lands of Great Britain and Ireland.

II.—THE AFFORESTATION OF IRELAND.

25. In the first part of this paper I have dealt with the forest question generally in respect of Great Britain and Ireland, and I shall now proceed to offer some remarks with special reference to Ireland, commencing with the consideration of the indirect effects of forests.

1. *Forests in relation to Topography and Drainage.*

26. Ireland has been described* as an island consisting of a great central plain, bounded near the coast by groups of mountains, though not entirely surrounded by them. Along the north, west, and south, the coast is deeply indented, and the central plain is intersected by numerous lakes and sluggish rivers, which find their way out to sea at the head of the bay and estuaries. A line drawn across the centre of the country from Dublin or Dundalk Bay, on the east, to Galway Bay, on the west, will meet with no higher elevation than that of about 250 feet above the sea, but a section in every other direction will be found to cross a mountainous ridge bounding at each extremity the central undulating plain. The mountains surrounding this plain may be divided into the following groups:

(1.) The north-western highlands of Donegal and Derry.
(2.) The western highlands of Mayo and Galway.
(3.) The south-western highlands of Kerry and Cork.
(4.) The south-eastern highlands of Wicklow and Dublin.
(5.) The north-eastern highlands of Mourne, Carlingford, and Slieve Gullion.

Many minor hill ranges exist, besides the above, but it would lead too far to mention them here in detail.

27. The central plain is described as being underlaid throughout the greater portion of its area by Carboniferous limestone, except near local disturbances. The limestone is only occasionally visible, as the greater portion of the surface is overspread by beds of limestone gravel, or boulder clay, or by shallow lakes and streams. Extensive peat mosses are a still more recent covering. It is believed that this limestone plain was originally covered throughout its area by coal measures, which denudation in the course of time has reduced to such an extent, that the originally vast Upper Carboniferous beds are now represented by only a few scraps left here and there. Coal-fields are found at Tyrone in the north, and at Killenaule and Castlecomer in the south.

28. The *north-western* and *western* highlands are formed of Lower Silurian beds generally converted by metamorphism into crystalline schists, quartzites, and gneiss. The highest elevation in these two ranges is reached at Muilrea, 2,688 feet above the sea. The *south-eastern* highlands are formed of Granite which penetrates Lower Silurian beds, the latter being considerably

* Hull, "The Physical Geology and Geography of Ireland," page 120.

metamorphosed; they rise to an elevation of 3,039 feet, at Lugnaquila. In the *south-western* highlands the rocks are disposed in long parallel bands, ranging nearly east and west. The narrower bands are formed of Carboniferous rocks, the broader of Old Red Sandstone; the former occupy the valleys and arms of the sea, the latter rise into mountainous tracts. These ranges include the loftiest elevations in Ireland, the ridge of Macgillicuddy's Reeks rising to a height of 3,414 feet above the sea. The *north-eastern* highlands are old volcanic, and remarkable for the number and variety of rocks and minerals which they possess; the highest elevation, Slieve Donard, is 2,796 feet above the sea.

29. Ireland is drained by 226 separate rivers, with numerous feeders. The following are the twelve largest drainage basins:—

	Drainage area, in square miles.
(1.) The River Shannon, in the centre and west,	6,060
(2.) The Suir, Barrow, and Nore, in the south-east,	3,555
(3.) The Bann, Main, Moyola, Ballinderry, and Blackwater, with Lough Neagh, in the north-east,	2,242
(4.) The Erne, in the north-west,	1,689
(5.) The Blackwater, in the south,	1,284
(6.) The Corrib, in the west,	1,212
(7.) The Foyle, in the north,	1,129
(8.) The Boyne, in the east,	1,040
(9.) The Moy, in the west,	805
(10.) The Slaney, in the south-east,	680
(11.) The Liffey, in the east,	529
(12.) The Lee, in the south,	484
Total,	20,709

These twelve basins drain about two-thirds of the total area, while the remaining one-third is divided amongst the other 214 rivers.

30. In addition to the rivers, Ireland has a large number of lakes, both situated amongst the mountains and in the plains. The largest of these is Lough Neagh, with an area of over 150 square miles, forming part of the Bann River drainage basin. The Shannon, in its course of 160 miles length, passes through a series of lakes; the Corrib and Moy include also large lakes in their drainage basins.

31. Although the principal mountains are grouped along the coast, Ireland has a distinct main watershed, low as it may be, which commences near Lough Foyle, runs through the centre of the country, and ends near Bantry. This low watershed divides the waters between the Atlantic Ocean and the Irish Sea.

32. After these premises I shall proceed to consider in how far afforestation is called for with reference to the regulation of moisture, and the prevention of floods and landslips. If Ireland was situated in a more southern latitude, or removed from the sea, its configuration would probably make afforestation a neces-

sity; but, owing to the existing climate of the country, all the waste lands in the lower part of the country, and along the lower and even portions of the higher parts of the hill ranges are naturally covered with a dense growth of heath, grass, and mosses, which act as most powerful retainers of moisture, and bind the surface soil together. Anyone, who has travelled in Ireland, must have noticed that this covering of the soil is, after rain, saturated with water to such an extent that the addition of trees would make comparatively little difference. Moreover, as already mentioned, afforestation would necessitate the artificial draining of a considerable portion of the land, and I am, in the absence of statistics on the subject, very doubtful whether the operation of afforestation would, on the whole, act beneficially as regards the regulation of moisture. The comparatively small additional effect of the forest growth would probably be neutralized by the draining of the soil.

33. The upper part of the hill ranges consists to a considerable extent of rock, much of which is at present bare. Here afforestation would probably produce some good effects, but the undertaking would never pay, and it could only be justified on public grounds, if the damage done by the rushing down of the rainwater was great. I have, during my late tour in Ireland, seen traces of such damage, but on the whole, it is not much. The rock is generally sufficiently consistent to resist any appreciable eroding action of the rain water. To sum up, as regards the denudation of the hill sides, afforestation is, in my opinion, at present not called for; at any rate the question is neither urgent nor very important, as long as erosion is not artificially assisted by the act of man.

34. It has been stated above, that the rain water which falls in Ireland is carried into the sea by 226 separate river basins. Here, then, is already a great division of the waters, which in itself prevents the occurrence of catastrophies like those which were reported some years ago from the valley of the Rhone in France. Some damage is no doubt done, but I feel satisfied that it will be much cheaper to face the loss which is occasionally caused by inundation, than to attempt its prevention by the afforestation of rocky hill sides. A good deal of relief has already been given by engineering works, and more can, no doubt, be done in this way, where necessary, at an outlay much more commensurate with the effect, than if attempted by afforestation.

35. Much capital has been made out of the effects of forests on sudden floods, and the afforestation of Ireland has been strongly urged on this ground, the drainage area of Lough Neagh being used as an illustration. I regret that I cannot support what has being advanced in this respect, because the effects of forests in Ireland have been decidedly over estimated. I shall attempt to illustrate this statement in the case of Lough Neagh.

The area of Lough Neagh is given as	153	square miles.
,, ,, drainage basin,	1,712	,,
Total,	1,865	,,
Proportion of lake area to total area,	1:12	

If 1 inch of rain falls within 24 hours, and one-third of it sinks into the ground or evaporates, while two-thirds reach the lake within 24 hours, the level of the lake will be raised by 8 inches minus what is taken away by the Lower Bann, or say 6 inches. Supposing 100,000 acres, or about one-twelfth of the drainage area, was planted with forest, and these planted areas retained twice the quantity of water, two-thirds of the fall instead of one-third, the level of the lake would thereby be reduced by $\frac{8}{12 \times 2} = \frac{1}{3}$ of an inch. If 250,000 acres were planted, equal to about 20 per cent. of the total area, the reduction of the level of the lake would amount to $\frac{1}{3} \times \frac{5}{2} = \frac{5}{6}$ of an inch. In reality, however, the effect would be much smaller for the reasons given above, and I doubt whether the planting of 500,000 acres, or about 40 per cent. of the total area, would, during a fall of rain of 1 inch within 24 hours, reduce the level of the lake by more than 1 inch. Moreover, it is, in several instances, not clear to me how the areas to be planted are to be obtained. It has, for instance, been proposed to plant in the basin of the Upper Bann river an area of not less than 51,200 acres (80 square miles), but I find that the whole county Down contains only 51,158 acres of waste lands. Assuming that of this area 30,000 acres are situated in the Upper Bann drainage basin, and that of these 20,000 acres are found fit for planting (a most favourable proportion); it would be necessary to take at least 30,000 acres out of the grass or cultivated lands, an inroad on the food and fodder resources which could scarcely be justified or approved. Armagh, again, which adjoins county Down, and is situated in the Blackwater drainage basin, has only 15,739 acres of waste lands, and here also planting could only be done on a limited scale. On the whole, I believe that it will be wise to leave the case of Lough Neagh, for the present, in the hands of the engineer.

36. I trust that I shall not be misunderstood. Where unafforested waste lands are generally bare of vegetation, afforestation will have a powerful effect, but where such lands are covered with a growth of heath, grass, and mosses, as in Ireland, an effect similar to that produced by afforestation is already in existence, and the addition of trees will not appreciably increase it, especially if the planting must be accompanied by the artificial draining of the ground. I fully believe in the beneficial effects of forests on the regulation of water as a general principle, but I demur to the application of that principle without due consideration of the special circumstances of each country.

2. *Forests in relation to Climate.*

37. Ireland is situated between the 51st and 56th degrees northern latitude, and the 5th and 11th degrees western longitude; it is surrounded on all sides by the sea, and subject to strong wind currents, more especially along the western coast. The Agricultural Statistics of Ireland for 1884, contain detailed data regarding meteorological observations made at Dublin (at 51 feet

above the sea), during the years 1864 to 1884, from which I have compiled the following table:—

Season.	Annual Average of 20 Years' Observations, 1864-84.			Observations of 1884 only.		
	Temperature, in Degrees Fahrenheit.	Number of Rainy Days.	Rainfall, in Inches.	Barometrical Pressure, in Inches.	Tension of Vapour in the air, in Inches.	Relative Humidity of the air, in Per cent.
Spring,	46·9	46·6	6·048	29·873	·260	77·4
Summer,	58·4	47·8	7·338	29·980	·393	76·8
Autumn,	49·3	48·5	7·626	30·068	·313	84·0
Winter,	41·4	51·7	7·003	29·845	·238	84·5
Mean or Total of Year,	48·9	194·6	28·015	29·942	·301	80·7

The temperature, measured 4 feet above the ground, is given as deducted from the maxima and minima readings of the thermometer by Kaemtz's formula:—

$$[\text{Min.} + (\text{max.} - \text{min.} \cdot 41) = \text{mean temperature}].$$

Spring comprises here the months of March, April, and May.
Summer " " " June, July, and August.
Autumn " " " September, October, & November.
Winter " " " December, January, & February.

The mean or totals of the year are correct, as given in the Agricultural Statistics, but the means for the four seasons have been calculated from the means of the several months, and they are, therefore, liable to slight corrections; the differences, if any, are, however, small.

38. The wind directions, according to the observations made in 1884, are as follow—if the numbers given for north-west are equally divided between north and west, those given for northeast equally between north and east, and so on:—

West winds,	41	per cent.
South winds,	28	,,
East winds,	15	,,
North winds,	11	,,
Calm,	5	,,
Total,	100	

39. Dublin is situated on the east coast, and its climate does not represent the average of Ireland. Data, similar to those given above, for a station on the west coast are not at my disposal, but sufficient is known to justify my stating, that the rainfall on the west coast is much heavier than that at Dublin, and, it may be inferred, also the relative humidity of the air.

The following data shows the rainfall for a number of stations:—

Cork, annual average of 1860–80,			. .	36 inches.
Waterford,	,,	,,	. .	43 ,,
Kilkenny,	,,	,,	. .	43 ,,
Armagh	,,	,,	. .	31 ,,
Antrim,	,,	,,	. .	35 ,,

The average rainfall for all Ireland has been calculated to range from 38 to 40 inches a year.

40. Compared with continental European countries of equal latitude, Ireland has a comparatively small range of temperature during the different seasons of the year, a low temperature during summer, a high rainfall, and a damp atmosphere. It follows that the tendency of forests to reduce the temperature, to increase the relative humidity of the air, and also perhaps the rainfall, is not only not required in Ireland, but that it would be actually injurious if it were not very small compared with the action of moist sea winds. In this respect, then, afforestation is not required in Ireland.

3. *Forests in relation to Winds.*

41. The action of forests on winds and the protection which woodlands afford to cattle and useful birds deserve great attention. It is well known that the strong sea breezes which sweep over Ireland, especially along the western coast, impede to a considerable extent the successful prosecution of agricultural operations, and any measure which would reduce this baneful effect must be beneficial. I do not advocate the planting of a *continuous* long belt of forest along the western coast as has been suggested, because such a measure seems to me actually impracticable, and if practicable and carried out it would protect the fields behind it only for a certain distance, when another belt would be required for the fields further inland and so on. I believe, however, that much good could be done in this respect by a judicious distribution of forest blocks over the country, more especially in the coast districts, without attempting to create continuous belts.

42. The protection which forests afford to cattle is also highly beneficial in a country like Ireland. I have been assured that Scotch farmers pay, in many cases, twice as much for the grazing in forest lands as in open lands; not because the former yield more fodder, but because the cattle thrive better, owing to the protection which the trees afford to them.

4. *Forests in relation to Wood Production.*

43. The question of wood production has been dealt with in the first part of this paper. It is only necessary to repeat here that Ireland is rich in peat, and that coal can be laid down at a low rate; hence the production of firewood is at present of little or no importance. On the other hand, I have attempted to show, that the production of timber is likely to pay fairly by the time

forests now planted are ripe for the axe, provided the work is done in a judicious and economic manner.

5. *Forests in relation to Labour.*

44. It has been shown above that forests, if established on surplus lands, bring additional work to the people of a country, not only through their ordinary administration and working, but also by the springing up of a variety of industries connected with forest products. It is evident that the consideration of this question must be of importance to a country like Ireland, where the following remarkable facts face each other:—

On the one hand, Ireland has large areas of waste land, which could easily be converted into useful cultivated tracts;

On the other hand, the population of Ireland has steadily decreased during the last forty years, chiefly by emigration, in round figures from eight to five millions; even now emigration continues; a certain number of agricultural labourers seek, during part of each year, work elsewhere; and generally a good deal of poverty prevails, especially in the coast districts.

What is the cause of this? Here is a problem which has been, for years past, one of strong contention in political circles. It is not my intention, nor have I any desire, to discuss the Irish question generally, but, in order to deal with afforestation in relation to labour, I am constrained to offer a few remarks on it, with due deference to those who are better qualified to judge.

45. It has been said, that the Irish rural population is lazily inclined; but it is also well known, that the Irishman is a first-class workman, when employed elsewhere. Why should he work hard in England, and why not in Ireland? Surely only for this reason, that it pays him to do so in the one case, and not in the other. Emigration has, even of late, been encouraged. To get rid of a number of troublesome people may be very convenient for the moment, but such a measure cannot produce any lasting good effect; to establish peace in a country by depopulating it is, of course, opposed to all sound principles of national economy. As long as waste lands fit for cultivation are available in a country, emigration should be discouraged and not encouraged. The cause of the evil must be looked for elsewhere, and the cure attempted by other means. It cannot, for a moment, be supposed that Providence made the Irishman essentially different from those around him; there must be some cause inherent to the country in which he lives, which has by slow degrees, made him what he now is. This I believe to be the peculiar climate of the country combined with the state of proprietorship of the land. Nature has produced the former, the act of man the latter.

46. According to the present state of affairs, the ordinary Irish cultivator is expected to earn a livelihood for himself and his family, and to pay rent to the proprietor of the land. If the

climate of the country was more favourable for agricultural pursuits, than it is, the cultivator might be able to meet both demands permanently; in reality, and especially in the poorer parts of the country, he gets on fairly well in good times, but he breaks more or less down in unfavourable times, because the surplus earnings of good years are not sufficient to carry him safely over bad times. In other words, the climate of a great portion of Ireland is not sufficiently favourable to produce crops, which will permanently support the tenant and yield large rents to the proprietors of the soil. The consequence is that the tenant, not having sufficient interest in his holding and consequently in the peace of the country, is easily persuaded to agitate, and the proprietor must forego his rents in a greater or less degree. Could the cultivator *by fair means*, be converted into the owner of the land, his means would be greater by the amount of rent now paid, and he could live with his family and be in a better position to weather unfavourable years. Above all, he would have a substantial interest in the peace and quietness of the country, and he would soon learn to turn a deaf ear to the words of the agitator.

47. The Legislature of this country has clearly expressed the intention of assisting the Irish tenants to become the owners of the soil, which they cultivate. The last Land Law (Ireland) Act of 1881, contains provisions to regulate the rents chargeable on land, and to facilitate the purchase by the tenants of their holdings under certain circumstances and conditions. Section 26 of that Act empowers the Irish Land Commission to purchase any estate for the purpose of re-selling to the tenants comprised in such estate their respective holdings, if the Land Commission is satisfied with the expediency of the purchase, and is further satisfied that a body of tenants not less than three-fourths of the total number, and who pay in rent not less than two-thirds of the whole rent of the estate, are able and willing to purchase their holdings. The condition as to three-fourths of the number of tenants may be relaxed on special grounds, with the consent of the Lords Commissioners of the Treasury, but in no case shall the number of tenants, who are able and willing to purchase, be less than one half of the total number. The Act provides further, that the Land Commission may sell any parcels of a purchased estate, which it does not sell to the tenants thereof, in such manner as it thinks fit; the Land Commission may also advance up to three-fourths of the purchase money to any tenant who buys his holding, the sum thus advanced being recovered in instalments.

48. I understand that, although many proprietors would be only too willing to sell their estates, little advantages has, up to date, been taken of the facilities offered to the tenants to become the proprietors of their holdings. This is, no doubt, to a considerable extent due to the acute agitation at present prevailing in Ireland, but partly also to the difficulty of disposing of whole estates. A few tenants may offer to buy their holdings, but the proprietor naturally hesitates to dispose of these, perhaps the best, holdings, and have the rest, in a cut-up condition, left on

his hands. Again, the Land Commission cannot act unless three-fourths, and under special circumstances one-half, of the total number of tenants are able and willing to buy their holdings. This limitation was, apparently, inserted in the Act, because the Legislature did not wish to encumber the Executive Government with extensive areas which might be left on its hands, and from which no suitable returns could be obtained. It is here, that afforestation may become an useful auxiliary in solving the Irish land question, especially in the poorer parts of the country. Assuming that more extended powers were given to the Land Commission, and it bought a large estate, say in Connemara or Mayo, it would proceed to sell to the tenants as many of their holdings as they were able and willing to purchase, and perhaps sell additional parcels to outsiders. This operation should be conducted on the principle of "give and take," and suitable compensation, if necessary, given for rights in outlying parts, so as to round off the area disposed of. Of the remaining lands some may consist of holdings, the tenants of which are neither willing to purchase, nor would it be advisable to evict them, and they would have to be kept for a time, as Government tenants, until they became able and willing to acquire their holdings, or give them up; but if the proceedings are conducted on the right lines, it will doubtless be possible to reduce their number to a minimum. All lands then left in the hands of the Land Commission, which would be principally situated on the hill ranges, should, in my opinion, be converted into State forests, as far as they are fit for the purpose. The surplus lands would represent only a comparatively small portion of the purchase money, as they would comprise the less valuable parts of the estate. In this manner Government would be able to utilize all surplus lands in an economic manner.

49. It has been said above, that agriculture in Ireland does not yield returns sufficiently large to enable the cultivator to live and to pay rent permanently, and now it is proposed that he shall, over and above, purchase his holding. The task is of course beset by great difficulties, but I believe that it can be accomplished, if the State recovers the purchase money under the system of a sinking fund, calculating the annual payments with the rate of interest at which the State can borrow money, and if, in the poorer districts some additional work can be provided, which enables the new small proprietor to earn something in his spare time. If the State is determined to take steps which will go at the root of the Irish difficulty, and effectually interfere in the land question in the manner indicated above, the result would be, that the annual payment, under the system of a Government sinking fund, to be made by the cultivator, would little, or not at all, exceed the rent which he has now to pay, owing to the low interest at which Government can borrow; the cultivator would not be worse off than hitherto, and after a series of years his payments to Government would cease altogether. In order to pilot him safely over the transition period, additional work is required, and this must be of such a nature that it will fit in with agricultural requirements. Ordinary industries will, as a rule, not

do this, because they produce a separate class of workmen, who devote themselves to the special work. Afforestation of the surplus lands, on the other hand, will be found to suit the case. Every acre of land planted with forest will involve an outlay of £2 to £3 in wages, which can be earned by the surrounding population; and after the forests have been created, work connected with their management and forest industries will replace that provided by the original planting. Excepting the duties performed by the administrative staff, the work connected with forest operations can be done when agricultural operations are slack, and the small cultivator can take advantage of every spare day to earn a day's wages by work in the forest, or by devoting it to simple forest industries, and thus increase his income and capability of meeting the annual payment when it becomes due. The labourer can in most cases live in his own home, and he can put by the whole of the extra earnings; this is of great importance, for if he had to go to some distance for extra work, he would have to spend a great part of his earnings before he returned home. I believe that, as regards the solving of the Irish land question, and through it the ultimate restoration of peace and quietness in the country, the afforestation of surplus lands, especially in the coast districts, will be found of considerable importance.

50. Dr. Lyons, Sir Thomas M'Clure, and Mr. Maurice Brooks prepared and brought into the House of Commons in 1884, a Bill for the re-afforestation of the waste lands of Ireland, in which it is proposed to accomplish the work through the agency of occupiers of waste lands, tenants of land for statutory terms, owners, Boards of Guardians, and Government. This is as it should be; but the returns from newly planted lands are so distant, and the plantations have to be closed against grazing for such a long period, that tenants are not likely to render much assistance. More may be done by proprietors, though many will be unwilling to invest further funds in Ireland, and others may be unable to do so. Something will probably be done by Boards of Guardians, but in many cases, I feel satisfied, Government will have to take the initiative. Objections might be raised to Government becoming in this way the proprietor of extensive lands, but I do not propose that it should interfere, except in those cases in which present proprietors are unwilling or unable to keep the matter in their own hands. At any rate Ireland has now drifted into such a condition that some sacrifice must be made. Much weight has also been attached to the springing up of forest industries, these are not likely to be created unless the supply of the necessary forest produce is regular and sustained. There is no guarantee that this will be the case as long as the woodlands are all held by tenants and private owners; for this reason it is necessary that at any rate a portion of the forest area should be under the permanent control of Government.

6. *Area available for Forests in Ireland.*

51. In the first part of this paper I have given the general distribution of the land in Ireland; it will be useful to add here

a somewhat more detailed record of it. The Agricultural Statistics of Ireland for 1884 give the area of waste lands as follows:—

	Statute acres.
Bog and Marsh,	1,738,751
Barren Mountain Land,	2,164,403
Water, Roads, Fences, &c.,	850,332
	4,753,486

This total does not include an area of 494,726 acres under the larger rivers, lakes, and tideways. The area of 850,332 acres under water, roads, and fences, &c., may be at once left out of consideration; there remain then 3,903,154 acres. Assuming that one-half of this area is fit and available for planting, an area of 2,000,000 acres in round figures (= 3,125 square miles), could be converted into forests. The above areas are distributed amongst the several counties in the following manner:—

County.	Bog, Marsh, and Mountain Land.		Per-centage of Grass Lands to total Area.	Per-centage of Land under Crops to total Area.
	In Statute Acres.	In Per cent. of the Total Area.		
Donegal,	508,502	43	33	18
Mayo,	545,915	41	40	13
Kerry,	381,694	33	49	13
Galway,	459,897	31	50	13
Sligo,	109,030	24	51	19
King's,	117,664	24	47	23
Tyrone,	183,637	24	42	30
Wicklow,	117,955	24	49	21
Waterford,	97,574	21	52	18
Cork,	334,418	18	54	22
Londonderry,	90,872	18	42	35
Leitrim,	60,992	16	54	23
Longford,	40,896	16	52	26
Roscommon,	86,330	15	59	22
Clare,	109,102	14	61	19
Antrim,	83,931	12	51	32
Tipperary,	120,354	12	58	25
Queen's	46,724	11	53	30
Fermanagh,	44,822	11	59	23
Kildare,	39,651	9	59	26
Westmeath,	40,989	9	64	20
Down,	51,158	8	39	46
Cavan,	37,425	8	54	30
Louth,	15,179	7	39	46
Carlow,	15,708	7	54	34
Limerick,	46,363	7	62	26
Wexford,	35,280	6	53	35
Dublin,	13,493	6	50	35
Kilkenny,	26,802	5	59	28
Armagh,	15,739	5	40	49
Monaghan,	13,583	4	48	40
Meath,	11,475	2	70	22
Total of all Ireland,	3,903,154	19	51	24

52. In the above table the counties have been arranged according to the proportion of waste land to the total area. It would be beyond the scope of this paper to examine in detail the points on which afforestation depends, nor would it be possible to do so without a minute examination of each locality, but, in a general way, it may be said to be governed by the extent of waste land and its proportion to the total area. The proportion of land under crops to the area of grass land is also of considerable importance. Donegal, Mayo, Kerry and Galway head the list just given, their per centage of waste land ranging from 43 to 31. The proportion of land under crops to grass land in all Ireland is 24:51, or about 1:2; in the above four counties it is as follows:—

In Donegal,	18:33
„ Mayo,	13:40
„ Kerry,	13:49
„ Galway,	13:50
On the whole about	14:43 = 1:3

Under these circumstances it may be assumed that the greater portion of the waste land in these counties, amounting to 1,896,008 acres, could at once be made available for afforestation. At any rate, I feel sure to be within the mark by counting on 1,000,000 acres, or scarcely more than one half of the total waste area, which would be distributed somewhat in the following way:—

	Statute Acres.
In Donegal,	250,000
„ Mayo,	300,000
„ Kerry,	200,000
„ Galway,	250,000
Total,	1,000,000

Sligo is likely to provide 50,000 and Cork 150,000 acres, while the remaining twenty-six counties would be able to contribute the remaining 800,000 acres of the total estimated area of 2,000,000 acres, without trenching to an appreciable extent on the fodder resources of the country. The afforestation could only be carried out by degrees, and the areas would not be closed against grazing until they are actually taken in hand. After the forests have been created, only about one-third of their area need be closed at one time, the other two-thirds being available for grazing. Here, then, is a field for action, whether it be undertaken by Government, corporations, proprietors, or tenants. The returns which the waste lands yield in their present condition are, on the whole, small, and afforestation could, I have no doubt, be made to pay fairly, apart from the benefit which the people in the poorer coast districts would derive from the increase of work afforded near their homes, and the protection which the forests would give to the adjoining fields and to cattle.

7. *Organization.*

53. If it should be decided to carry on afforestation in Ireland on an extensive scale, it will be necessary to provide a central authority, which can direct the operations on the right lines. The Bill for the "Re-afforestation of the Waste Lands of Ireland," mentioned in paragraph 50, proposes the following organization:—

(1.) A fit and proper person, eminent for his knowledge and skill in the science and practice of forestry, shall be appointed to be Chief Forest Conservator for Ireland.

(2.) Five persons shall be appointed to be Commissioners of Forestry for Ireland, of whom one shall be the Chief Commissioner of Works for Ireland for the time being, one shall be the Vice-President of the Local Government Board, one shall be the aforesaid Chief Forest Conservator for Ireland, and two shall be such persons, one eminent in the law and one eminent for his knowledge of forestry, as the Lord Lieutenant shall select and appoint, and who shall be willing to act as unpaid Commissioners. These five Commissioners shall constitute the Forest Department of Ireland.

(3.) The Forest Department of Ireland, as constituted above may, with the consent of the Treasury, appoint a Secretary, and such Assistant Forest Conservators, Inspectors and other necessary Officers, as the Treasury shall sanction.

54. The principal duties of the Irish Forest Department are described in the Bill as follow:—

(a.) The Forest Department may acquire by purchase, or rent for terms of years, suitable lands for forest purposes, wherever forests may be required for shade or shelter, as wind-brakes, for the protection of agricultural land, for the control or regulation of the water supply, for the preservation of the soil, for the remedy of floods and torrents, or for the improvement of any other of the physical conditions subservient to animal or vegetable life.

(b.) The Forest Department may, in the same way, acquire suitable lands with the view of increasing the forest area of Ireland generally up to one-fourth or one-third of the total area, and constitute such lands State forests of Ireland.

(c.) The Forest Department may accept the temporary assignment of waste lands for the purpose of re-afforesting them, or it may undertake the care, management, and felling of any forests growing on lands so assigned to it, or the care, direction, and management of any existing forests in Ireland.

(d.) Wherever floods and torrents prevail in Ireland, the Forest Department may institute an inquiry by competent Officers into the nature, origin, and extent of such floods and torrents, and prepare a scheme for the effectual remedy of the same. The proprietors and occupiers of such a flood district may be summoned together by the Forest Department, to constitute themselves into a syndicate for the purpose of carrying out the scheme proposed by the Forest Department. On the neglect or refusal of the proprietors and occupiers to constitute such a syndicate within twelve months, the Forest Department may apply for an order to the Local Government Board to enter on the said lands, and carry out the necessary operations at the expense of the proprietors and occupiers of the lands.

(e.) The Forest Department shall furnish any Board of Guardians in Ireland, carrying out re-afforestation operations, with a detailed scheme for the planting operations most suitable to the locality to be planted, and depute an officer from time to time to inspect and report on such works.

(f.) The Forest Department may establish a School of Forestry for Ireland, conduct examinations in forestry, and confer diplomas in forestry.

55. These provisions cover the principal ground. What final shape the organization would have to take depends on the results of Irish legislation, which, I understand, is now pending. There will, under any circumstances, be a central authority in Dublin, to which a Commissioner for Forests could be attached. The Commissioner must, of course, be a person eminent in the science and practice of forestry, and he should be a member of a Board constituted on the lines given in the above mentioned Bill. That Board would be the Forest Department of Ireland. As regards the subordinate staff it is, at present, only necessary to say that the members must be carefully selected, so as to insure success at the start. Probably operations would be commenced in one or two localities only, and they would afford opportunity for training a number of young Irishmen, who could then be drafted to commence work in other localities.

8. *A few Sylvicultural Notes.*

56. The methods, according to which afforestation shall be carried out, and the species of trees to be planted must be determined and selected by the professional staff with special reference to the conditions of each place. I found everywhere evidence, not only of forests which grew in Ireland in former times and the remnants of which can still be seen in the peat bogs, but also that forests can be grown and will thrive in the present day. Even in the immediate vicinity of the west coast I saw well grown woods. Solitary trees are, when exposed to strong winds, much deformed, but wherever they are grown in masses and the

ground is well stocked, only those directly exposed to the wind are injured in their growth, while they afford the necessary protection to those standing behind them. The depth of the injured belt differs according to the force of the wind and the general exposure of the locality, but, under proper treatment, it need not be very great, and the loss of growth on this account would not be serious.

57. As regards the species of trees to be grown, I desire to add a word of warning. I have seen long lists of exotic trees, which are recommended for planting in Ireland. If anything of this kind were attempted at the outset, it would be sure to bring discredit on the operations, and I feel satisfied, that no forester of experience would countenance any such steps. The main stay of the operations for years to come must be the species, of which it is known that they will thrive and produce good serviceable timber in Ireland. After the business has been got into working order, there would be no objection to experiments, on a small scale, with exotic species which promise well, but I should deprecate any large expenditure under this head, until experience has proved that a species is suited to the climate of Ireland.

58. Of the indigenous and well established species, the Scotch fir will be the ruling tree in the dryer localities, and spruce in the moister places. Alder may be planted in wet situations, in so far as they cannot be used for osier beds. Oak and silver fir may be grown in suitable localities and soils. Larch will, on account of its quick growth and superior timber, deserve attention, provided it be mixed with other suitable trees in a proportion ordinarily not exceeding one in four. Birch will come in useful in many exposed localities, especially in protecting belts. Sycamore and other useful trees may be sprinkled into the forest in suitable localities. Beech is an exceedingly useful tree from a sylvicultural point of view, but it yields chiefly firewood; nevertheless, its cultivation should not be lost sight of, especially as some of the forest industries depend on the supply of beech wood.

More I do not desire to say at present under this head.

Before bringing this paper to a conclusion, I desire to repeat that it makes no pretension at being exhaustive. Still, it may be found to contain some remarks which will be useful in considering and solving an economic question of some importance to Great Britain and Ireland, and more especially to the latter country.

W. SCHLICH.

London 1st January, 1886.

Printed by Libri Plureos GmbH in Hamburg, Germany